WHAT IS TIME?

C.A. MacKenzie

Cyberwit Publishers
HIG 45 Kaushambi Kunj, Kalindipuram
Allahabad - 211011 (U.P.) India
http://www.cyberwit.net
Tel: +(91) 9415091004
E-mail: info@cyberwit.net

Printed at Thomson Press India Limited.

CONTENTS

WASH AWAY

I scrub and scrub,
trying to erase stains gravelled upon my face.

Age has defined its mark,
solidified a presence in folds and furrows
raked over a once-smooth fabric now heralding me as old.

These seams line my skin,
years claimed my youth
from time I hadn't known had passed
and disappeared too fast
like thieves in the night
creeping without warning.

I smell that newness born with babes,
Oh, how it escapes me,
leaving soiled flesh in its wake.

I'm alive,
still breathing,
but it's sighs of old.

Vibrancy and youth permeate my spirit
until the mirror silently highlights worn flesh,
illuminating my face and
haunting me like a ghost
forever lurking around me.

When I peer closer I see more yet less of me,
fragments of remaining years shadow daylight gone,
like dirt disappearing from a child's face in the rain,
innocence turned to the sky,

tongue gathering pearls.
Age is dark. Quiet. Unobtrusive. Unwelcoming.

These common threads live to capture us all.

WINTER'S DEAD HOSTAS

I wrench the dead from thawed ground
to allow blooms to emerge,
yanking hollow stalks,
snapping thicknesses in two,
bending spongy ones,

I pile parchment-like meshes of leaves
once moulded tight beneath the snow,
bittersweet and moist, but now ready to go,
life ending as it does every spring,

The blood seeps and I try to quash it,
as I've tried to stop the flow before,
pale stalks lay in piles,
war-time bodies waiting for burial,

I gather the dead in my arms and enter the woods
where I gently lay them upon nettles
and dried leaves to find life again
after they fragment and disappear into the soil,
melding into earth from whence they came,

I caress those fallen timbers,
limbs that stained my hands bright red,
while I mourn another year gone,
time lost forever, never to be recaptured,

Our bodies lay like those old stalks
when we are laid to rest,
we disintegrate too and families mourn
while we return from whence we came.

ONLY ON PAPER

Poets scrawl words, painters splash colour
on paper meant to be viewed;
A driving force propels senses
of time, imagination, foreboding;
Focused in the moment, life escapes,
fear evaporates and dries our eyes,
chases our demons,
quashes our breath;
Waves crash upon the shore
threatening to drown us in tears;
Monsters create shadows from within
to drag us to another world;
We watch and wonder
of the whys and the wheres
and dream of long ago
people, places, periods;
Life happens before we die,
visions overcome us and
threaten to destroy our souls;
We live within the mist and the downpour
and the wild winds blowing across the seas.

THE FICKLE FLAME

We can't control God's candle,
That flickering flame,
When it's lit or dies.

We celebrate birthdays,
Insert candles into cakes,
One to ninety-nine
The years are immaterial
Except to the birthday person
When he or she
Blows
And blows,
Sometimes one breath
Sometimes two
Or more...

Who cares
As long as the flame is gone,
The wish wished
And cheers and accolades spewed.

Birthdays come but once a year
When wishes should come true
and flames should glow forever

Young or old,
We think we're invincible,
That death will never find us,
That we can hide in a closet
Or behind a keyboard
Or behind a tree—
So many places to hide—

But when death comes calling
There's no place to hide.

We are gone.

Gone.

You are gone,
I am gone,
He and she...gone!

God knows, though.

Only God knows our end
And we can't bargain
Because when death comes
It's too late for, God's already taken us
And He can't undo what's been done
And prayer can't undo what's done.

Perhaps at birth
Our deaths are ordained,
No accidents,
No twists of fate,
No nothing...

Death is what it is...

Death... just is.

But not for death
There'd be no life
For death can't exist without life
And life can't exist without death.

A FAÇADE

You attempt to hide behind
your façade of bricks,
layers piled high between the mortar,
but your soul seeps through the cracks
as the mortar weakens over time,
and the bond,
once boldly red,
is now an ugly grey
aged by time and death.

FLOWERING DREAMS

She gathers dreams in her arms,
Held like a dozen long-stemmed roses
Freshly cut from the garden she tends,
Each blossom caressed by her fingertips
As if garnering strength with which to cope.

Beautiful flowers of varied colours,
Unlike wild roses and shades of her life
—some dark and empty—
—some bright and full—
And she yearns for those times.

But she knows they're over,
That life dealt a cruel blow
And no matter the words she hears
They won't be enough to keep her domain intact.

Her world will turn without her,
One body out of millions
Won't be missed except by her.
It's like a wooden peg yanked from a clothesline,
Fallen upon the grass,
Broken in two, trodden and beaten into the soil.
No one misses the clothespin.
No one will know she's gone.

She steals a breath,
Inhales the delicate scent of flowers
Resting in her arms,
The baby's breath whispers, "I love you,"
While prickly thorns pierce her tender skin.
She shrieks, laughs, weeps,

The flowers drink her tears
And absorb her weakness.
Petals spread and the centre of the blooms
Rise to view her
As if giving thanks
For the fluid of survival.

Green stems reach and twine about,
Smothering, drawing her in,
And the rush of their desire devours her
And sweeps her into dreams,
Those dreams she once held in her arms.

FLIRTING

Little birds flirt
not knowing who they hurt,
"Sing with me," one calls,
"I'm not breaking any laws."

He's like a little bird
flitting to and fro.

"Dance with me," he begs.

"No," I say. "I can't."

STEALING TIME

I try to find you
Whether you're hiding
Or lingering

The cold silence rushes in
Unannounced
When I think calm will prevail

It's unexpected
Like the hush at death
When a face is at peace

A HIDDEN HOPE

Some days I long to stay in bed, yanking shrouds of silk
over my head, to live cocooned from the world and forget
burdens fallen upon me, a banished bird living in sordid
shadows.

I'm unable to continue a life unfolding day-to-day with
issues and conflicts too great to resolve, unable to
understand a passion thrust upon me.

I don't know where to run or where to escape, not wanting
to go but needing to retreat and hide among the masses, to
search for peace and tranquility grasped and held by
others, wondering why it's beyond my reach.

Friends and family not knowing or not caring, unaware of
the depths of my pain, and I ponder the wrongs and
inability to mend broken dreams.

I'm empty and lonely, dressed in my solitude, left alone to
cope and grieve, fears mingling with tears that beckon
breezes into my soul to shroud me in their form so I can
hide.

Thoughts and plans abundant of a future unsure and at
times lost in laughter and lollipops and embracing
innocent kisses and caresses, a certain calmness amidst the
storm though still yearning to escape, knowing it's only a
fleeting joy, a smidgen's squeeze of love and happiness, a
tenderness here today but gone tomorrow.

OF THE NIGHT

'Twas a dark night when I caught you there,
Twinkling stars highlighting your hair,
Coal black it was, the colour of death,
Though I glimpsed your snowy breath.

A silky dress flowed 'round shapely legs
Hidden under cloth like tables' long pegs,
Your face turned from whoever might see
You lingering there, happy without me.

You brushed away a strand or two
From your eyes once true and blue,
Where was he, your man of the night
Who caused my heartache and woeful plight?

I loved you with everything I possessed,
Our union was one that God had blest,
You forsook our life and what we had
For someone else, that worthless cad.

Who are you to decide our fate,
To fill me up with so much hate?
My love for you was ever true
And now you've made me very blue.

I will love you still if you return to me,
If you leave that wanton man and flee,
Come home to me, my dear, before I die,
Before you hear my endless sigh.

No longer can I watch you, nevermore
Standing 'neath a streetlamp like a whore,
My long-bladed knife hangs in the barn,
I can find it easily and spin a yarn.

A tale of woe so fine I'll never pay
For a horrible deed on such a gray day,
But never fear, my lovely sweet,
I'll remember you ever on the street.

We'll meet up again sometime
When my last bells rhyme and chime,
I'll tell you then how fine you were,
How you made a lowly heart stir.

He's gone now too, I did him in,
But no one knows my double sin,
I did it, I want to jump and shout,
But one good deed's enough to spout.

PAGES FROM THE PAST

Pages creak and cry when turned,
Reminiscences of old returned to life,
I read faint words,
Ponder the person who wrote them
And admire the fancy scroll of
The faded ink of the fountain pen.

No binding, no staples,
Nothing holds the sheets together
But accumulated dust,
A yellowed pile of memories,
Crinkling before they fragment,
Returning to the past.

A POT OF WATER

A pot sits quietly on the burner.
Water stagnant and fermenting
gradually simmers,
gently boiling,
rapidly boiling,
throwing itself into the air,
dropping sizzling shards onto the stove.

Anger is like mud
thinning in the rain,
a dark steady stream flowing into the sewer.
Tears and rain,
hidden,
droplets wet upon cheeks
unleashing a torrent,
a flood of emotions,
a release of feelings.
The sewer a receptacle
catching the aftermath.

Anger is a bottle of champagne,
its feelings suppressed,
uncorked to release emotions,
high-spirited
with broken bubbles.

Anger is fireworks
soaring into the sky,
exploding above us,
awakening the heavens
and powdering the air with colour.

Anger is a like a computer
crashing,
losing its information,
its mind,
collapsing in a heap,
worn and exhausted.

Anger is like a vehicle
careening out of control.
Not caring who is there,
not caring who is crying,
a runaway train,
a thief in the night.

Anger is thunder and lightning,
sharp daggers through the heavens,
touching earth,
bold shouts,
screams in the night,
lashing out.

Anger is a snowstorm
tossing white through the air,
dropping cold upon earth.

Anger is like night
falling upon day.

Anger is a raging bull
running to the red,
enticed by shouts,
goaded to its task.

Anger is cancer
ravaging the body,
taking all it can,
leaving nothing left.

Anger is a volcano
lingering beneath the earth's surface,
biding its time,
waiting to erupt.
Words lying in wait to vent,
to spew,
to discharge.
Combustion gathering its steam,
exploding into heat and light.
Waiting minds crack under stress and strain.
Future mountains waiting,
To be climbed and overcome.
Fury unleashes wrath,
bringing tears of torment
and actions of rage.
The furious fire burns through the night,
a storm of madness raising the roof.
Red sparks of fire spew to the Heavens,
then fall back to Hell.

Anger is water,
a boiling process.

ONE TOGETHER

You and I lie still together,
Bound as one without a tether,
Tightly linked, no dull space,
Staring eyes shine face to face,
Our mouths near, an inch apart,
Once latched, nevermore to part,
We will share each other's breath
Until the end, our ultimate death.

While we breathe upon our souls
A healing heat fills up holes,
Our chests thump in rhythm firm,
Legs intertwine, not to squirm,
Arms enfold around each other
Careful not to bruise or smother,
Fingers caress upon flesh
Warm and inviting as they mesh.

Comfortable and softly smooth
Is our touch that doth soothe,
Calmness upon us negates a pain
That over us doth sometime reign,
For we are one and we are two,
Our forever love always new
And for all eternity we will live
Within a passion that we give.

A MOMENT

A Moment
To stop
Watch
Listen
Feel
Smell
Touch

A moment's
Hesitation
This or that
To ponder
Reflect
Appreciate
Share

A Moment
In time
A cry
A laugh
A breath
A sigh
Death

A Moment
That's all
To hug
Hope
Love
Live
Die

TO BE A KILLER

On a dark and eerie night
Under stars not so bright,
Roams a man with a plan
To kill as many as he can.

He's a serial killer, as yet unknown,
Who kills those lives on loan,
People unaware, enjoying lives,
While he decides on guns or knives.

His weapon of choice becomes a gun,
Knows it's fast, they can't run,
Corners them wherever he can,
Doesn't matter—child, woman, man.

He sees their fright, eyes so wild,
Likes them to cower, meek and mild,
It's easy then to execute,
He does it for fun, there's no loot.

Police are after him, that he knows,
At the scene, doesn't linger or pose
Where he feeds on his prey,
Taking them as he can, in any way.

Needs another, three or more,
Anything less would be a bore,
He hangs his trophies on a wall
In his head where they won't fall.

He's gotta be sneaky and oh so quick,
Can't be choosey who to pick,
He knows they'll find him soon,
Perhaps before a fortnight's moon.

Leaving clues is not so smart,
As others before him, who did dart,
A copycat can't always win,
Not when deeds are done in sin.

No more, he thinks, *I have quit,*
I'll behave, before a TV I'll sit,
Perhaps unaware TV is worse,
Some of the shows can be a curse.

But a day without is hard to do
And he becomes so very blue,
His genes are bad, the way he's made
He can't stop, murder won't fade.

One more, he thinks, *just one,*
Then I'll prove that I have won,
Cops won't find me, I'll live free
Forever more, you wait and see.

He takes his gun and off he goes
To find someone he can dispose,
While crossing an alley, he sees her
Bundled up warm with a scarf of fur.

He grabs her arm to pull her in,
Into the lonely alley full of sin,
The night grows dim and dark
While he looms, like a shark.

Too bad, so sad, he is too slow,
Too unaware to deal a blow
Or use his weapon and leave,
Before she pulls hers, her pet "Peeve."

That's the name she gave her gun
Which she holsters every dawn of sun,
Always with her, saving lives,
Even fighting husbands and wives.

An undercover cop is she,
No one would know it, not you or me,
A disguise so great, she always passed
Scrutiny, wherever a net was cast.

He's seen her before, other times
When contemplating horrific crimes,
Watchful was she, hidden behind a mask,
Waiting for him to start his task.

Another person will not die,
Not while under her watchful eye,
Bound and determined is she
That he is done with every spree.

Gotcha, Bud, she does retort,
Come with me, gotta write my report,
Now you're done, jailed you'll be
For all time, you wait and see.

No, no, he says, *I'll get off,*
I've more people to find and boff,
He talks big, but deep down he knows
His days are coming to a close.

And sure enough, cop lady is right,
The jury sentences him up tight,
Never again will he roam or see
The light of day, nor ever be free.

SILENCED

He quashes dreams
Along with screams
When out of nowhere
He jumps to scare.

Fright comes later
Like a looming gator
When dawning appears
Along with fears.

He carries a knife
To end a life
Thinks he's God
He is too flawed.

Perhaps his past
Caused him miscast
And morphed a child
Into an adult wild.

Death happens before
An open door
That can't be shut
Before the cut.

Watches and grins
Despite his sins
The erupting blood
Streams into a flood.

Knows he's bad
Isn't even sad
It's in his genes
To cause these scenes.

More death to come
More minds to numb
One kill won't do
Not enough to chew.

He's a serial killer
Living a movie thriller
Taking great pleasure
At his leisure.

Hopes are dashed
Because of his past
He quashes dreams
Along with screams.

IN THE DARK

It's lonely in the dark
When I cannot see,
It's, oh, so dark
When I'm alone
Thinking of you
And no one knows.

In the dark
I cannot see,
In the dark
It's only me,
In the dark
I weep for you.

Oh, darkness,
Cover me
When it's light,
Don't let light
Force me to see;
I'd rather pretend.

In the dark
I cannot see,
In the dark
It's only me,
In the dark
I weep for you.

I miss you
In darkness and light
Whether my eyes
Are closed or open,

In the dark I cry
And no one knows.

In the dark
I cannot see,
In the dark
It's only me,
In the dark
I weep for you.

EVEN IN DREAMS

Stop. Stop. Stop.
I chase after him
But I grasp only air.
He's gone...

I screech
(in my dream).

A nudge on my arm.
"Are you okay? You okay? You okay?"

I wake.

"I'm fine."
I'm fine. I'm fine. I'm fine.

I roll over
And cry.
Cry. Cry. Cry.

Even in dreams
You break my heart.

WHAT IS TIME?

What is time
But passing rhyme,
Breath,
Death.

Illusion of space,
Running the race,
Limbs that move,
In the groove.

A loving embrace,
A lonely chase,
Hearts that beat,
Friends who meet.

Tidal waves,
Stalactites in caves,
Serenading song,
Ding, dong.

Seconds, minutes, hours,
A dream sours,
Sand in the hourglass,
Thru the looking glass.

A new week,
Straining to seek,
Undiscovered days,
A different phase.

Out with the old,
In with the cold,

Shouldering storms,
Until life warms.

Sweating the heat,
Pluralize cheat,
Open your eyes,
Catch the lies.

Stars in the sky,
Moon hanging high,
The setting sun,
Day is done.

Oh, what is time
But passing rhyme,
Hands on the clock,
Tick, tock.

ONCE UPON A TIME

Many years ago I saw you,
not too many, but a few,

Highlighted by a light
oh so huge and bright
that soared from the moon seeking
a path to Heaven, as a peeking
light fell upon the wildflowers,
casting reflections of showers
upon your lovely face
of such supreme grace
shining bright,

You clad all in white
standing among fanciful flowers
in the early hours,
colourful circlets like faces
humbled by gentle embraces
while looking to the skies
emit wee sighs
of happiness for the morrow,
but your face is one of sorrow,

Fate made me stop that night
before I knew of your plight,
when I breathed in the scent
of the endless garden's lament
and that of you
and your last debut,

Then everything stopped,
flowers dropped

and you cried
and all died
except the love in your eyes
that was ill-disguised
until the angel appeared
—just as I had feared—
to lead you home
before the whispering dome
could crush the skies
to hush its lies,

The heavens bowed down
upon you in your white gown
and lit up the skies so blue
to delineate the path before you,

And you were there no more
for you had gone thru the door,
no more would I see sorrow
etched in your eyes on the morrow,
no more would hate meld
the glow of love you held
for you went home
no more to roam,

And the light dimmed forever more
upon the land's great shore.

THE FINAL CURTAIN

Upon the canvas I sketch your face,
Hair I draw, features I trace
Cover youth that time did erase,
Seams that remained after life did race.

When you were young, time did withstand
Particles of dust that dared to land,
Many seeds upon your face and hand
Now reveal years that time did brand.

I display the painting to your scrutiny
But I'm not trying to pull a mutiny.

There's no privacy, your age is there,
Crevices and crannies you now wear
Are on display to those who stare,
Time takes all, no one's youth to spare.

I speculate at lines I've drawn,
Those that appeared before the dawn,
I see your tears at that night's yawn
Shrouding a face that will soon be gone.

A cloth can cover peoples' scrutiny,
But death remains to pull a mutiny.

WANTING

I want so much
To hold and touch

You are there
But I grasp air

For before I move
I need to prove

To myself at least
That you have ceased

Your wanton ways
Throughout the days

The lies you've told
Have left me cold

And I need time
Before I climb

Back to the stair
That place so rare

Where I dare
Grasp more than air

WAVES OF MADNESS

We bare our breasts before diving into the depths. In the dark it's warm, yet we are chilled. It's the plunge that does it. The suddenness takes our breath until the cold overtakes and numbs us and we think we're warm.

We spread our arms and embrace vast waters as if flying through layers of billowing silk on a hot summer's day. Or maybe it's our bodies unwrapping from layers of inhibitions and shame, floundering through waves fierce and loud.

There's no life preserver. Our choices are limited and we think we're drowning—may even want to drown to avoid suffocation in seaweed.

We see sharks as we move, forcing ourselves to stretch our arms and kick our legs. We hold our breath without swallowing, and when we drink it in we spit it out so we don't choke.

We swim another lap and another and another while embracing tides tamed in our hearts, thankful we took the plunge because it was all we could do other than die and disappear.

We wanted to live and keep ourselves safe before waves covered us forever...

These waves of madness reach for us all in the end.

"ANGRIALITY"

Frowns of fury transform a face.
Hot tempers
and quick tempers bristle.
Bodies change and collapse,
react in fear
with split-second decisions.
The welting whiplash,
charging chains.
Objects careen through thick air.
Pain and control.
Right and wrong.
A partner no more,
alone in the day and night.
Abuse of the mind,
abuse of the body,
too physical in the fight.

The thief enters at night,
knocking down doors,
pirating and plundering,
taking what is not his.
Stealing hopes and dreams,
leaving nothing in return.
Grabbing whatever he can,
his fortune to make.

A man taking what is held dear,
an irreplaceable part of a soul.
A criminal,
a sexual deviant.
Ruination of a human being.
Incest through the years.

A brazen assault,
unnecessary.
A woman left to endure forever
what a man stole.
Ravishing the beauty.
Raping the soul.

The madman stalks.
He's a lunatic, a maniac.
Crazy rage,
unnecessary.
Killing and murder.
Ending life, not caring.
Tears forever.

A stranger enters the room,
playing a dangerous game
of passion and deceit,
love and hate.
Desire.
A hunger for devotion,
beauty, love, money.
Living in the moment,
not caring who is hurt.
Regret comes later for the pain.

Curses chewed and spit.
Stinging accusations of mistrust,
and minds gone wild.
Lies.
Words that sting and control.
Words that cannot be withdrawn.
Words that endure.

Reality comes to call.
Where to turn?
Who is there?
Seething in the pit of their being,
a soul tarnished and worn.

Angry reality of life.

CHANGE OF SEASONS/THE TREE OF LIFE

The tree of life grows,
How far it goes
and where it goes
no one knows,
Its branches separate
and spread,
outstretched like fingers splayed
and reaching to the sky
as if grasping air and life,
Buds sprout,
leaves growing
green and fresh,
living for a season
in the sun and rain,
dying when day is done,
Pulled by gravity
to the ground,
remains resting,
scattered when blown by wind,
searching for
its final resting place,
Earth to earth,
ashes to ash,
dustings to dust,
back at peace,
buried in the soil
awaiting rebirth
as the seasons
change again.

HOMELESSNESS

He's cold and much does he bear,
More than clothes replete with holes,
Torn and tattered and threadbare,
And dirty shoes with worn soles.

His face is framed with matted hair,
An etching of another life,
His hands folded as if in prayer,
Knotted and gnarled with strife.

The streets have been his home
For longer than he can remember,
Through many a town he did roam
From January to December.

Once he sought his elusive dream
But it was never meant to be,
And many a time he did scream
For his God to set him free.

He's hungry today as in the past
And doesn't see an end in sight,
If he hadn't been proudly steadfast
He could have helped his plight.

Pride flows through every vein
But being proud won't keep him alive
Nor keep him warm or feed his pain,
Unlike most of us who thrive.

He'll remain on that park bench
Until the police drag him away,
They'll put him in a cell of stench
Where he'll survive another day.

SNAKE EYES

My insides coil and recoil
like a serpent spiralling
through my spine
and I cringe at the pain
—and you.

Your snaky eyes
glow in the dark
before your mouth opens wide
to spew venom
onto my face.

I wipe it off,
calmly,
while you watch
behind your veneer
of viciousness.

Acidity boils
through my veins,
yet I rein it in,
not letting it out.

A heavy weight crashes on me,
overpowering me
as I twine about you
and collapse within myself.

And I see a thousand stars
shining in the sky.

FAITHFUL (HERE BESIDE YOU)

I'm here beside you,
In front of you,
Behind you,
Day in and day out.

I see what you do,
I glance at you
Or stare from afar
And take a peek.

I hear your voice,
Your whispers and shrieks
Buried in truths and lies,
Your secrets.

Often you don't know
I hear,
Other times you don't care.

You hear me talk
But don't listen,
You don't digest my words
Or feel my pain.

You see me
But don't look,
You don't notice tears
Or fear in my eyes
Or white upon my cheeks.

I touch your pain
Amid laughter,

I caress love and hate
And feel your embrace.
I smell your desires
And ambitious thirsts
For covetousness and charity,
Fragrance and foulness.

I taste your tears
Of joy and sadness,
Bittersweet and savoury,
And relish the flavours.

I'm in front of you
Or behind you
Or at your side,
Always here.

HIM

My sights are on him
—the photo in the magazine—
and I grip it tighter
—the gun—
for that face
—though not really him—
is a trigger
that unleashes emotions
I thought were gone,
and the anguish
is like a hammer
forever pounding
upon my heart.

MY DEAR R,

Tonight is just for you and me
For us to share in revelry,
We'll stare into each other's eyes
Illuminated by stars in the skies.

Forever we've wanted time
For our bodies to rhythm in rhyme,
We'll sway to music in our ears
As we hide deep-seated fears.

Like a simple hammer and nail
Our unhappy hearts will flail
And collide happily together,
Light as a single feather.

We'll caress and touch
With abandon, perhaps too much
Forbidden fruit excessively sweet
In the passion of a heartbeat.

Alone to discover each other
Our breath we will smother,
Perhaps we'll pause to wonder
If we're making a huge blunder.

Fingers succinctly, carefully
Will travel bodies soft and woolly,
A time of exploration with exploitation,
Culminating from past flirtation.

The glancing sparks will fly
When you clasp my thigh,
In return I'll grab hold of you
Experiencing something new.

We'll proceed in discovery mode
With our pasts safely stowed,
It'll be love—or will it be lust
That upon us will be thrust?

Whatever its name, it's forbidden
And we must keep it hidden,
That's what dreams are made of:
A wild abandon love.

With glee we'll share passion
In feral unfathomable fashion,
Moving as one, feelings of two,
Collapsing when we are through.

We'll shiver in the night's dark
At the suddenness of a spark,
Sensations hidden far too long
Heard only recently in song.

We'll forget our daily troubles
While soaking in floating bubbles,
We'll sip sparkling champagne
And forget the year's past strain.

Our secrecy of deceit and lies
Might hide forever in our eyes,
Neither of us will be the same
After we play that shameful game.

We should end it before it starts,
Before too many unknowing hearts
Are broken with the real truth
And lose innocence from youth.

But we've already betrayed another,
Somewhat like crucifying a mother,
Let's seek answers within our soul
And leave each other whole.

But, no, we don't want to stop,
Not yet, we've barely reached the top
Of our emotions and passions to share
That part of our souls we want to bare.

The words I desire to tell you
Are not words that we are through,
Oh, how I wish we could escape somewhere
So your fingers can linger longer in my hair.

But tonight will be for you and me
When neither of us will run nor flee,
We'll stare into each other's eyes
Illuminated by stars from the skies.

Love, Carmen

ONE RED ROSE

One red rose is all I want,
laid by my head as I sleep,
my body's frail and gaunt,
I'll be fine, don't you weep.

Memories I will keep,
trembling, I'll forever haunt,
emerging from the deep
one rose I will flaunt.

I know you'll nicely taunt,
prodding my soul to keep,
but I'll fondly take a jaunt
to watch o'er you as you sleep.

One red rose is all I want
laid upon us as we sleep,
over our bodies gaunt
one red rose will surely weep.

MY HEART

My heart given to you that day
was a shaped stone found
upon the ground,
delicately, I brushed it off
and held it out to you—
a gem formed over time,
cold and hard as steel,
yet warmed with love and peace
from my hand to yours.

PAINT AND SHADOWS

The painted portrait coloured by wedded bliss
hangs upon a small hook, decorating the wall,
eyes stare into a future that will hold memories.

Two faces,
young and fresh and innocent,
with hopes and dreams and plans and goals
share their past
and now share their future and fortune
together as one.

Sixty years later another portrait hangs in its stead,
images of lines and shadows
drawn from years of living and wedded bliss,
framed by the glow of burning candles,
a shadow of two lives living together as one.

And then there is only one life left,
alone, the cord cut
and breath stopped amid precious rain,
memories of a life lived with another,
and one doesn't forget while watching from above,
blowing love in the breeze
and hiding kisses in the raindrops,
expressions of wonderful wedded bliss.

Two framed portraits now united as one love,
forever and ever,
eyes watching still, encompassing all,
hang above the mantle upon small hooks,
two old souls' hushed voices in the night,
dulled by the flame and reunited once more in love,

kissed by raindrops and caressed by autumn leaves
falling upon the concrete slab.

LOVE OF TWO PEOPLE

Love is a lifetime of laughter and sharing,
A lifetime of loving and soul-baring.
Two people fall in love and marrying,
Full of hope, promise, and caring.

Love is a dream of promises to fulfill,
Lingering thoughts and prayer to instill.
Two people with a dream, each with a will
To make the other happy, calm, and still.

Love is a word with a definition so fine,
Everyone wants it, all of mankind.
Two people together looking for a sign
Of happiness forever, their love to shine.

Love is a feeling, a place of escape,
Great emotion, a rush that does drape.
Two people caress, a kiss on the nape,
One life to live, two loves to shape.

Love when it dies is never a good time,
People's lives are shattered, cry and whine.
Two people then, they do long and pine
For the good times, when it was fine.

WHAT IS HOPE?

Hope is a flavour of emotion, a sweet dream of
tomorrows, fleeting wishes of desires.

Hope is a burgeoning fire,
flames searching the dark,
futile yet real.

Hope is sad, a blissful tease,
temptation, a thrill, a rainbow of colours
streaking across the sky.

Hope is a prayer of love
and laughter, purity and perfection, happiness and
honesty.

Hope is a scream of sorrow
and serenity, of strength and struggle, salvation under
shining stars.

Hope is an olive branch,
a peace offering, a white dove searching.

Hope is a wishing well
strewn with pennies,
tossed in expectation
and wonder.

Hope is a courtship, a promise of lies and truth,
fraught with emotion, tender in the night.

Hope is a gambler
throwing cards in anticipation, in trepidation.

Hope can be a fantasy,
positivity or false hopes,
daydreams and nightmares,
circumstances beyond control, a pipe dream.

Hope is a field of dreams
in spring, bulbs emerging,
reaching for the sky, searching for life.

Hope is opening a book
and turning pages,
reaching new chapters,
tomorrows of optimism,
savouring words, hoping for more.

Hope is a path of life,
enticement for the future.

Hope keeps life living
amid death to come.

I LIKE WATER THAT TASTES LIKE WINE. AM I OUT OF LINE?

I drink wine
From the fridge
Like water
From the tap.
Bottle or box,
One glass or two,
I don't care or count.
Each glass disappears
And refills
Like magic—
A miracle!

All that keeps me alive these days
Is that which hastens my death.
But in the moment
The amber dulls my pain,
Let's me forget,
Allows me to dream
And pretend,
To don my make-believe mask
And smile like a lipsticked clown:
A frightful frown
Hidden behind a disguise,
Where I can pretend all is okay,
That you are still here
And you'll walk through the door
And ask how I am,
"Anything I can do?"

"No, sit down," I say.
"Have a break. Want a beer?"

FOETUS

a chance meeting
in the dark,
two strangers:
cells—
egg and sperm—
forming one,
a thimble of life

thriving inside,
growing,
yearning,
grasping air
as it yawns
and punches the barrier,
kicking,
wanting to exit,
not realizing its creation
veiled
in the cocoon

it hears the music
and listens to the words—
eavesdropping—
not knowing,
forming preconceptions
as it vibrates
in its camouflage,
demanding its first release

THE STAR

The night is hollow and cold,
and I'm alone in blackness;
I've never liked the dark,
don't like what I can't see.

Stars are funny creatures,
resting and hiding by day;
They emerge at night to party,
when their florid faces glow.

They glare at us, those stars,
spying upon us in the quiet;
And we stare back at them,
desiring futile fantasies.

I've never liked the dark,
don't like what I can't see;
I beg and beg upon one star,
please let my wish come true.

TIME IS RHYME

What is age but a passing rhyme,
Minutes and hours merging in time,
Seconds depleted without a breath
Bring us all much closer to death.

We don't see time that seems to fly
By faster than the blink of an eye,
It's invisible, hidden within air,
Perhaps taken with the sun's glare.

We can search and search 'til day's end
For that elusiveness around the bend,
But we'll never find it nor capture it,
No matter how fast we race or flit.

DEATH

It rips at your soul,
Clogs your pores,
Dulls your senses,
Grips and won't let go.

It intrudes into your life,
Disrupts your existence,
Causes the sky to blacken
And clouds to burst.

Even when expected,
It's a thunderburst of agitation,
Upheaval, and empathy,
A gut-wrenching tug of emotion.

It's a heartbreak like no other
For those left behind,
For those close and near,
Why, Death, oh why?

FLOWERS OF LOVE

You send me flowers for Valentine's,
cut flowers, colourful and fragrant,
beautiful—
and they brighten up the room
and my day,
but they soon die:
they wither and dry,
their leaves brown and
the petals darken
and fragments fall to the floor.

Yet, they can be pretty, still,
as dried flowers,
and if you don't touch them
they won't shatter and turn to ash.

We can be like flowers—
strong one day
and fragmented the next
when we are touched by life and time—
but we will endure,
our two lives will exist as one
whether we are together or apart,
for we were meant to be,
like perennial blooms of flowers.

THE SEAMSTRESS

My mother holds the tangled threads of her five children
Gathered in her frail hands,
Now adults, all of us,
Yet her babies still,
Siblings once woven so tightly.

She clutches the flimsy threads delicately,
Not wanting them to break,
But she knows when her time is done
The stitches,
Brittle with age,
Will pucker and snap,
Unravelling like a knitted sweater frayed at the seams
That slowly unweaves and shrinks in the wash.

The five of us,
Once finely patterned within the squares of a cosy quilted
comforter,
Are now knotted differently,
We are mismatched buttons,
Different paths we stitched,
Different worlds we embroidered,
Different blueprints we followed.

We may have been pierced with needles or cut with
scissors
And discarded like scraps and rags
But still forever entwined,
Criss-crossing like lattice or unfolding like yards of white
lace
Or glistening like beaded brocade,
Other times jumping through fitted hoops casting each

other off.

Sometimes we're bold like strands of gold and other times
We hide in the folds as we try to patch our souls.
We are twisted and at odds
The five of us—
Two against three, three against two—
Faded appliqués of various shades and sizes
Torn from a worn and loving quilted spread,
Smothered with pinpricks of jealousy,
Looping alone and spinning yarns and piping warped
dreams
That don't gauze the rip nor mend the tear.

We've forgotten the wicker basket from where we came—
A hamper once filled with love and accessories with
which to mend—
The one the seamstress hovers over,
Ever watchful and caring.

But in times of crises—
When pockets are picked and seams are shattered—
We gather and braid together,
Our dyes run forth while we weave our tapestry of colours
Into a padded patchwork that frames our mother in love.

ALL THESE THINGS

They say your memory's the first to go
but mine's still here,
and who is "they" anyhow?

I know my bones are decaying
and my body's weaker
but my memory's still here.

I look at my children—
and my grandchildren—
all adults now—
and wonder where the years went.

Was just yesterday
when I was young like them
but now I'm where my parents were
and where my grandparents were
when I was the age my children are now
and my grandchildren,
and I never thought I'd age this old—
this fast—
and now it's time to downsize
and I have all these things I cherish
and hold dear,
things I cannot take with me,
things my children don't want,
things my grandchildren don't want.

How did I get this old
with my mind still strong,
with all these things meaning so much to me,
these things I can't give away

because they're worthless except to me,
yet I can't throw them away
because they're my memories—
my past,
my life,
and my parents' past,
and my grandparents' past.

These things are me.

And where have my parents' memories gone
and my grandparents' memories?
Who holds those?

Is it only me?

My children don't care about memories
and things that aren't theirs,
they don't care about the past.

Is it just me?

Am I wrong
clinging too much
to what I know is fleeing
and fleeting
and soon to be gone,
wanting to grasp
and hold tight
to my life
and my past
and my memories
that no one wants but me?

A BLANK CANVAS

I gather tools in front of me:
paints and canvases and brushes

to paint a portrait
from a photograph of a face
I know so well
and love even more,

I discover wrinkles
and crinkles
I did not acknowledge before
for I did not see them,

and now,
like tears and unravelling stitches
upon a worn and dulled tapestry
they seem to mock me—
rich brown spots loom
and cryptic creases and mysterious furrows
race off to nowhere,

and I don't know where death ends
and where life began,

and I don't know how to proceed
for I don't know how to draw time
and paint passing years
that disappeared with barely a breath
before I knew they were gone.

A PORTRAIT OF MYSELF

I love to paint my grandchildren
—many portraits of pink and blue—
One painting didn't look like my granddaughter,
But I kept at it though,
Comparing her photo to the painting
I scrubbed her golden hair
and blued in more of her big eyes,
I reshaped her little pug nose
and moulded her chubby cheeks in pink,
I scattered tones of beige and white upon her face
—highlights to enhance the form—
When suddenly I realized I was looking at myself
when I was her age so many years ago.

BREATHE

She looks down upon him,
her husband of sixty-odd years,
prone on the sterile bed,
crisp white sheet drawn to his chin,
weary eyes closed and muted mouth agape,
breathing heavy,
then shallow,
grasping at life amid whispers of death,
a mind entombed within,
lost and floating,
floundering and shrouded in mystery
as he lingers
while she waits
and watches and wonders
what a mind thinks when it is gone.
After it disappears where does it go?
Do we ever wake to find our life gone?

FOLDS OF DEATH

Death erased the folds
that time lay upon you,
The caresses of love
sent from God above
wiped away your sins,

His tears healed your sores
and kisses eased your pain,
While resting you are free
from charades of life
and sorrow and loss,

For eternity He'll care for you,
Where you're in a better place,
But your memory
will reside forever
in our hearts and minds.

TIME

we live our Life as if at Play
waiting around for Death
not knowing what Death looks like
nor what it feels like when it's gone
but knowing it will come.

we never thought of Death when younger
not something we ever feared
but when we reach a certain Age
we realize Death is closer
and we cannot prevent Father Time
from catching up to our Day.

why didn't we do more
when Years stretched before us?

Time seemed Timeless then.
Life seemed Forever.
Years seemed Endless.

now there is much we want to do
and years remaining are few
why didn't we think of Death when younger?
instead of thinking we were Immortal
that Time would never catch up to Life
and we would Live Forever
and Death would never find us.

don't we all remember waking up
to view aged parents
knowing we would never reach that age
nor ever be that old?

we knew our grandparents were old
but that was okay because grandparents are old
and when they die that is okay
because all grandparents die
and we as little children back then didn't really care
because we knew they were old and supposed to go.

as children, Time seemed endless
stretched far
without care and worry
the rest of our lives ahead
and all the Time in the world
to do everything we couldn't think of then
that back then we didn't care about.

we aged some
and started doing more
but still thought we had unlimited Time
to Love and Live and Laugh
to discover Dreams
to fulfill Fantasies.

then one day we woke up
to find we are older
that we are parents
and our children look at us
the way we looked at ours
and our children think how old we are
the way we thought back then
when we would never be that old.

and then we are grandparents
and Reality moves in bringing Today
and we realize Father Time will soon come

'cause he's set his sights on us
and we don't have much Life left
and we know all the things we want to do
but not enough Time to finish them all
and we struggle to turn back the clock
to keep our children and grandchildren close
so they won't grow any more
so they can stay the same
so we can stay the same.

we make amends for our Past
and smother our grandchildren
doing for them what we never had Time
to do for our kids
how back then we didn't have Time to Play
not as much as we would have liked
now that we remember.

today we're retired
and called Old Geezers by some
with days free to devote to grandchildren
to give them Friendship and Love
but we know there's limited Time left
and we realize they won't care when we are gone
just as we didn't care when our grandparents left
because they were old
because it was their turn to go
because their Time had run out
and the Clock had stopped ticking.

HIDDEN

The flower's root hides underground
In another form.
It is a bulb
Small and round,
Waiting for the magic of birth,
Careless,
Soaking moisture
From the rain
And lapping vitamins
Of the land,
Biding its time
But soon to emerge,
A wondrous sight to see—
The emerging of the baby stem,
The green that forms into
A flowering beauty—
Beloved and cherished,
Cherished and loved.

RIPPLES

She sits on the sand
watching the water
as it ripples
through and through,
the tide bringing it in
and taking it out,
her memories
of people and places
and things.

BABIES

Unaware of thieving time
and shadows stolen in the night,
Not understanding fancy voices speaking
nor knowing the breath of buffoons
or the fear of fools,
Not seeing the clowns' comic monotony,
the giggles of glee,
nor feeling the faith of followers,
Not hearing the silence simmering through the world
nor seeing the glance of grimaces across a face,
Not hearing the cries creeping through the canvass
nor whispers and warnings of secrecy and hate
or bargains made in passages of sin,
Needing only warmth of shelter
and sunshine
and a hug's caress,
a gentleness of kiss
and release of hunger.

DESPICABLE DEATH

I wake in the dark,
Bleak black, stark,
My heart beating *tick tock*
And glance at the clock,
The hands point to five,
He didn't survive,
I let out a soft sigh
And stifle my cry…

Four months ago
The wind did blow and
Montreal was storming
At two in the morning
When to the hospital we raced,
Not ready to face
His failing breath
That might bring death.

We watched him die,
Prayed to Him in the sky,
We touched his legs
Stiller than pegs,
Too many alarms
While rubbing his arms.

His chest didn't heave,
I wanted to leave.
I wanted to stay.
Oh, how I did pray.
I could barely speak,
My body and mind weak,
Our voices did chime

In shock at the time,
While throughout the chill
His body stayed still.

We hovered three hours
Despite crying showers,
I saw his lone tear
Exposing his fear,
And after Despicable Death
Took his last breath
We lingered in the hall,
Leaned against the wall,
Sat on the hard floor,
Fled thru the revolving door.

Back in the frigid cold
On the ice we rolled,
Heading to Tim's
Where we sat on weak limbs,
Ate breakfast sandwiches
While brandishing
Hot coffee and Coke.
I almost did choke
How could we eat
When a heart failed to beat?
*How can we sit here
Not shedding a tear?*

I felt empty, cold,
And, oh, so old,
My son, my son,
I'm sorry Death won.

BUTTERFLIES

I chase the butterfly through the grass
Running after it under the skies
Darting here and darting there
Trying to catch it in my grasp.

That was years and years ago
When I was small and young
Today I'm older and wiser
Still chasing butterflies through the grass.

RAINBOW ACROSS THE SKY

The rainbow arches across the sky,
Beckoning me to follow the ray,
The colours are many, so bright,
Enticing me with the colourful sight
To leave this earth and stray,
As I hear the clouds' gentle sigh.

The end of the ray within our sight,
The arch circling up then down
To reach the sky then back to earth,
Playful and joyful in its mirth
As it touches its tip onto the ground,
After the rain in the bright light.

And so we find there is no end
To the rainbow colourful and bright,
Nowhere to take us under its spell
For it is on earth that we do dwell,
And when day is done it folds at night,
Waiting for rain, its rays to unbend.

THE SMELL OF DEATH

It's the taste of death we smell
When someone is aged and nearly gone,
The scent that lingers about them,
Wafting to and fro,
An odour so atrocious we plug our noses lest we
suffocate,
And we don't breathe again until we've left the room.

You can't mistake it—
That smell—
It can't be hidden,
It's distinctive
And everyone recognizes it,
Most everyone's smelt it.

It's the stench of old people—
Everyone knows that—
It's a horrid smell.

But is it truly the smell?
Or is it the import—
The nearness, the significance,
The idea it might be contagious, that the smell could
emanate from you sooner than you expect, sooner than
you want—that death could come calling for you?

They say once you breathe death you never forget it.

It's a smell that lingers forever.

BOSTON CREAM DONUT

Stuffing my face
With a Boston cream
Tastes like a soft dream
Sliding down smooth
My heart to soothe,
Satisfying urges deep
But makes me weep
Filling that empty space.

For it's not hunger I fill
But the hole in my heart
And I don't know where to start,
It's an empty void
Of things to avoid,
A void I need to complete
And so I cheat,
Stuffing that inner chill.

Once that's done
I am unsated but stuffed
And my belly's puffed
From eating instead of crying,
Giving in rather than denying,
And I want even more
Even though I swore
I'd eat only one.

A SIMPLER TIME

I'm more colourful than black and white,
more exciting than stories in the newspapers
delivered to your door with too many traces of gloom,
although with maybe a hidden surprise or two.

I'm as bold as Christmas ornaments shiny upon the tree,
glistening in the night like the stars up high,
so far away, yet so close, not easily touched,
so tragically breakable if knocked upon the ground.

I'm not as dainty as sheets of tissue that crinkle easily,
a covering like clothing to hide treasures and happy
delights,
but all too familiar with the paper's creases and crinkles,
deep crevices from too many years of work and worry.

I'm not as scenic as a drive through the highlands
from whence came my seed hundreds of years ago,
borne from ancestors I'll never know
but can only dream and wonder of their past lives.

Were they more interesting than me?
Did they love as easily?
Were their lives simpler
and less hectic in their time?

UPRISING

The steam rises from the ground
In the early morn—
Hot melding into cold—
The rush like a swarm of bees,
Crushing, electric, static,
Buzzing in the damp, waiting...

By day
I linger and watch
And wonder,
Captured by the essence of you
While withering into a cacophony of nerves
And hearing whispers from the trees.

The cold hard steel of your form
Descends upon me at night when
I envelop you with my veiled love.
I hide behind mascara lashes
And fear the hush of
Fallen angels hiding below.

THE MASK

You bury your hurt
Under your shame,
Hidden beneath bruises
And scars you mask
With makeup paler than your face.

Eventually makeup fades,
Disappearing,
Unnoticed,
Revealing the real you—
An imposter.

Void of cover-up,
What do you do?
You've bared your soul,
Revealed your true colours
And they may not be pretty.

You flounder in the luminous light
Striving to hide your features,
Knowing you're ugly and stark,
But the glare illuminates all
You've tried to make invisible.

There's no hope.
You are what you are.
Time displayed itself
And your secrets are unveiled.
Too late to don another mask.

ONE LAST KISS

Kiss me once
before I go.

Hold me tight
as I breathe
in your scent
and you
breathe mine.

One last time
let me linger
in your senses
before I wander
into another mirage.

PILLOW 'ROUND YOUR HEAD

Pain becomes unbearable
As you try not to weep,
Life's not the same,
A burden you can't keep;
Your head sinks into the pillow,
Your days numbered
And you try hard to live
Though when death arrives you must give in
When pain's too great;
And when you know it's time
You'll shut your eyes
And shed one last tear
And pray for better things.

You're old, what life is left?
Shouldn't you just go
Before the falling of next year's snow
So you can leave in warmth?

I watch you there—
Pillow framing your head,
How easy it would be
To smother life from you
And end your world today;
What difference would it make
If your life I did take?
You're already gone.
Aren't you?

I feel the pillow soft about you
In sharp contrast to your skin of leather,
Such lousy weather!

Let the rains begin
And parties enjoyed in sin;
Something possesses me
Like the devil rising,
Won't be my fault.

Money rests beside me
In the guise of waiting death—
Your body lank and dull,
Oh, the quandary, I do mull;
My hands reach out once more
To your sleeping form,
The heave of your fallen chest
Barely there, hushed at night.

Will you see the morning light?
Or will you face the golden light?
Both we do fear.

My hands are rigid over you,
Frozen in time;
Do I possess the strength of mind
Despite my strong arms?

My hands I slowly lower
With an evil force possessing me;
Not me. Not I.
I couldn't do such an act,
Too much tact have I.

But that evil force persists,
Enters my body
And stands me tall,
Encompassing my all;

My mind elsewhere
Counting coins
And stacking bills up high;
Your money—
The roots of all evils,
That flagitious force grabs my breath,
Am I dying too?
No, I'm still alive
And stronger than ever;
That force within eats away my good
And my fingers speed to your throat
And I press;
Your eyes open wide
And stare at me,
Your mouth forms my name:
"My son, my son,"
You mutter in vain,
I cannot bear to look.

I snatch the pillow from under your head
And cover those glistening eyes
Which no more will stare at me;
I move the pillow from your face
Not looking at your closed eyes,
Oh, dear mother of mine
How could I do such a thing?
For I loved you so;
It were the devil possessing me
And now I weep
And clutch my chest
For those eyes of yours are open wide
And your skin is soft as lamb
And your voice is velvet:
"It's okay, my son, I forgive you ever,

But my revenge will be so sweet,
There is no money, you see,
I gave it all away.
I saw that glint in your eyes long before my death was
due,
Bad you'll always be and were."

I clutch my heart once more,
It's beating...
I force it out and throw it at you—
Those eyes now closed forevermore;
My bloodied hands scrape across your face
Drenched with my tears,
In weakness I lie down beside you
And my heart;
You caress the mass carefully
Not wanting to bloody your hands,
I kiss your lips
And wrap my arms about you
Cleaving to you in death
As I did at birth.

ABOUT THE AUTHOR

Catherine A. MacKenzie escapes from her self-perceived mundane world by writing fiction and poetry. Although she dabbles in all genres, she invariably veers toward the dark. Her mother once asked, "Can't you write anything happy?"

Cathy's stories, essays, and poems have been published in many print and online publications. She has also published several short story collections, books of poetry, and children's picture books. ***Wolves Don't Knock*** is Cathy's first novel. ***Mister Wolfe,*** the darkly dark sequel, was published in 2020. ***My Brother, the Wolf*** will follow in 2022.

She is a member of several local and online writing groups, including the Evergreen Writers Group and The Spot Writers.

Cathy also edits, formats, and publishes other authors' books under her imprint, MacKenzie Publishing.

She lives with her husband in West Porters Lake, Nova Scotia. Her amazing, gorgeous grandchildren provide much joy and inspiration.

Cathy's collections include:

short stories:
Between These Pages
Paper Patches
Broken Cornstalks
Women: Wise, Wicked, Worn
The *Creepy Crazy Christmas* series of books
Hidden Places (YA)

poetry:
A Woman's Lament
Lovely Love and Tearful Tears
A Grandmother's Love
Once Laughter
Love and Laughter
My Heart Is Broken (It Needs Fixing)

novels:
Wolves Don't Knock (2018)
Mister Wolfe (2020)
My Brother, the Wolf (2022)

CONNECT WITH THE AUTHOR

Email: writingwicket@gmail.com

Blog/website: https://writingwicket.wordpress.com

Facebook:
https://www.facebook.com/cathy.mackenzie.790

Facebook "Writing Wicket" author page:
https://www.facebook.com/writingwicket

Amazon.com Author Page:
http://www.amazon.com/Catherine-A.-
MacKenzie/e/B006HSUD9W

Twitter: @GrannyMacKenzie

LinkedIn:
https://ca.linkedin.com/pub/catherine-
mackenzie/24/15/a5b

MeWe:
https://mewe.com/i/cathy.mackenzie